MW01640322

O Death, Where is thy Sting? O Grave, Where is thy Victory?

When God Speaks!

Be Blessed
Mr. Snyder

Vernon M. Henderson

VERNON M. HENDERSON

WestBow Press books may be ordered through booksellers or by contacting:

WestBow Press
A Division of Thomas Nelson & Zondervan
1663 Liberty Drive
Bloomington, IN 47403
www.westbowpress.com
1 (866) 928-1240

ISBN: 978-1-9736-6191-7 (sc)
ISBN: 978-1-9736-6192-4 (e)

Library of Congress Control Number: 2019907062

Print information available on the last page.

WestBow Press rev. date: 7/31/2019

Now when Joshua was by Jericho, he looked up, and behold, a man was standing opposite him with his drawn sword in his hand, and Joshua went to him and said, "Are you for us or for our adversaries?" He said, "No; rather I have come now as captain of the army of the Lord." Then Joshua fell with his face toward the earth and bowed down, and said to him, "What says my Lord have to say to his servant?" The captain of the Lord's army said to Joshua, "Remove your sandals, because the place where you are standing is holy (set apart to the Lord)." And Joshua did so.

—Joshua 5:13–15 (Amplified Bible)

I give glory and honor to my Lord and Savior, Jesus Christ. The Lord has given me the strength and endurance to complete this book. It was during trying times that my life was forever changed.

My wife, Gerri, was my support as we served the Lord. The agape love she has shown during these challenging times has shaped my perspective on life.

God has been a tremendous advantage for us. I cannot thank him enough. "Whoso findeth a wife findeth a good thing, and obtaineth favour of the Lord" (Proverbs 18:22 KJV).

I'd like to give special thanks to the men and women of God who inspired me during this time: my pastor, Bishop Daniel Robertson; Pastor Raymond Luster; Elder Eric Thompson; Elder Derrick Maye; Elder Wayne Lynch; Overseer Robert Norton; and the prayers of the Healing Ministry at Mt. Gilead Full Gospel International Ministries and Liberty University, whose phone correspondence help lighten the load.

Special thanks to Pastor Lewis Yancey, who is a warrior in Christ when you need him.

Contents

Introduction

This is a true story about a life-changing event that happened almost two years ago. I came into contact with a demonic force, and God saved my life. It inspired me to write this book on all the things Christians experience and overcome when serving God, including pain, suffering, and joy. These are life lessons that are learned in hard times. The book will not only inspire a Christian audience but others who like to read inspiring stories. God's eternal presence has many dimensions.

The Jericho Leadership Institute

In 2008, Vernon M. Henderson founded the Jericho Leadership Institute.

Its vision is to reach out to all offenders who are in prison or jail or have been released, helping prepare men, women, and children to be productive members of their communities and to serve God.

Its mission is to bring offenders past and present into the saving knowledge of Jesus Christ, so they may establish a one-on-one relationship with him and can mature and succeed when released into the community.

The Institute strives to provide a means to restore the whole person back to Christ, which consist of his or her spirit, soul, and body. The Jericho Leadership Institute does this through Bible studies and counseling, Christian leadership classes, church services, videotapes, books, correspondences, hospital visitations, life skills, course curriculums, transitional needs, and by supporting correctional facilities in areas of need.

What We Believe and Teach

In the triune God, Jesus Christ is true God and true man. The Holy Spirit is a divine person. Salvation is provided by the blood of Jesus Christ. All have sinned and come short of the glory of God and need salvation. Baptism with the Holy Spirit is available to the believer: the personal and visible return of Jesus Christ; the bodily resurrection of the just and unjust. All those who receive Jesus Christ as their personal Lord and Savior are part of the church (the body of Christ).

The Jericho Leadership Institute is in the process of getting its nonprofit status.

jericholeadership.org

Chapter One

The Separation

In 2015, I was working at Chesterfield Juvenile Detention Home as a supervisor. During this time, I was on the midnight shift and had established the Jericho Leadership Institute. I'd been interviewed by Prince William Juvenile Detention Center about a job. It had been several months, and I hadn't heard from them, so I thought the process was over for me, but God is great and mighty.

One early morning around 3:00am, while at work, the Lord spoke to me. He said to clean out my desk and prepare to leave, so I did exactly as I was told. Two weeks later, I was offered a job in Manassas, Virginia.

I knew some of the outreach for the prisons would have to be curtailed. I asked my friend Brother Robert Norton to keep services going until I got settled in the new job. That first year I was on the midnight shift as a team leader and then was offered the day shift, in the same position a team leader.

During my second year I was promoted to shift supervisor. I was blessed and still trying to move things into place so I could get back to prison ministry.

But the next event forever changed my life. I'll never look at circumstances the same way.

On December 30, 2017, I was on my way to Manassas,

where I commuted two or three times a week. The weather was clear in Chesterfield, Virginia, where my wife and I live. I was driving along I-95 for approximately an hour and a half when the weather started to change, and I took exit 234 in Dumfries.

I hit black ice, the car went out of control, and I repeatedly hit my head against the steering wheel. That's when everything seemed to slow down as the car went down the embankment, through the trees, and toward a car salvage business. There was a separation of my spirit man and my natural man. It felt like I was in a bubble and someone else was driving my car. I was missing trees and headed for a gray fence.

That's when I saw death and what was going to happen to me. Death is one of the highest principalities that the devil uses against Christians. Death showed me that my car was going to flip into the salvage yard.

Death said to me, "You're tired, and you're at peace with what's about to happen. There's nothing to be afraid of about the situation. If it ends this way, it's okay."

All my strength left my body. I felt powerless, unable to move. It was surreal, because the devil was acting like a friend who was encouraging me to go through with what he had shown me, as if he was saying, "Go ahead and deliver your life over to me."

But, praise God, I had rededicated my life to Christ in 1989 and was involved in prison ministry since 1994. My spirit man spoke to me. Psalm 91:11 (KJV) says, "For he shall give his angels charge over thee, to keep thee in all thy ways."

The Lord has given his angels charge over us; in Hebrews it means he has ordered them to protect us from seen and unseen dark forces. Also, Hebrews 13:5 (NIV) says, "Keep your lives free from the love of money and be content with what you have, because God has said, 'Never will I leave you; never will I forsake you.'"

The Lord says he will never leave or forsake us. All this is taking place in this brief moment. During this time, I believe God spoke a word because it wasn't the same voice; it was more authoritative and on a different level. He said to me, "It's already done. Pick up your bed, and walk."

I knew I immediately had to face some challenges in my life. My physical body was in the car, but my spirit was in another dimension with God at the same time. The presence of God superseded my physical body in the car.

It was like being in two different dimensions. I heard a noise under my car that sounded like clawing. The sound was so intense; it felt like something was trying to get through the bottom of the car. The sound, like clashing of steel against steel, pierced my ears. The front wheels tried to roll over the fence, and the car tried to flip into the salvage yard but couldn't. The car jerked back and forth, as if something was preventing it from flipping.

I knew God's angels were protecting me. I was experiencing living inside the bubble of God's protection. Christians believe in God, but when you know God's way of doing things, it translates into a relationship on a different level.

The car was a total loss. The tow truck driver said it took two tow trucks to get it out. I was blessed not to have any broken bones, but I had a concussion, as well as back, shoulder, and neck pain.

During these moments for Christians, I now understand you can easily move into a spiritual realm with God. We are spiritual beings and must discern spiritual things from natural things. God's presence means he's already aware of our situations and circumstances. Everything we do or say in our relationship with God matters. Nothing is too big or small for God. We must make a commitment to serve him. God's grace is sufficient for us.

Chapter Two

The Process

In January 2018, the Lord again spoke to me. He said, "It's already done. Grab your natural man, and take him to where your spirit man is going." It was instinctual, but I knew I had to go through a healing process, so I began physical therapy three times a week.

One day at PT, during my session, my therapist was talking about the ring on my finger, my college hall of fame ring from Bowie State University. In 1975, we were crowned Independent Black College Football Champions. We went 9–1, and I had a pick-six for forty yards that year. In the midst of my pain, the Lord gave my wife and I an opening to minster to the therapist and pray for her. The message was that the Lord cares about you.

The next week, she said she'd thought the whole weekend about the words my wife and I had ministered to her. It was something she really needed in her life right then. How good is God when you hearken to the Holy Spirit in the midst of your need and he blesses others! Hallelujah!

Later, the physical therapist came to my wife because she wanted to get her prayer request in. The therapist was being counseled by her pastor, but when God has a message for you, it can come through anyone. Wow! God really blessed her socks off.

I was still in pain, unable to sleep, and having dreams about the accident. My death kept coming back into my dreams. In one particular dream, I saw my boss telling me three times to go back to working midnights.

After waking that morning, I knew in my spirit that I had to change shifts because of the pending challenges that I was about to endure. I emailed my boss to let him know about the situation and the change that I was requesting.

I was dealing with the accident and seeing the doctor, and on February 5, 2018, she noticed that my heart rate was up. My normal rate is between sixty and a hundred, and my rate was 149. I had chest pains and shortness of breath, was in and out the emergency room several times, and was unable sleep. Also, I was missing work.

I remember the message given to me. "It's already done. Pick up your bed and walk."

Two days later, my doctor referred me to a cardiologist. I went from his office straight to the emergency room at St. Mary's Hospital. There, I had a procedure to get my heart rhythm down.

The procedure didn't work. It was tried again and still didn't work. I was then admitted to the hospital. The doctors told me I had to have a procedure to get the heart rhythm back to normal.

The devil was trying another door, but he could not open it. Job 2:3–8 (AMP) says,

> The Lord said to Satan, "Have you considered *and* reflected on my servant Job? For there is none like him on the earth, a blameless and upright man, one who fears God [with reverence] and abstains from *and* turns away from evil [because he honors God]. And still he maintains *and* holds tightly to his integrity, although you incited me against him to destroy him without cause." Satan answered the Lord, "Skin for skin! Yes, a man will give all he has for his life. But put forth Your hand now, and touch his bone and his flesh [and severely afflict him]; and he will curse You to Your face." So the Lord said to Satan, "Behold, he is in your hand, only spare his life."
>
> So Satan departed from the presence of the Lord and struck Job with *loathsome* boils *and* agonizingly painful sores from the sole of his foot to the crown of his head. And Job took a piece of broken pottery with which to

> scrape himself, and he sat [down] among the ashes (rubbish heaps).

I felt that my spirit was bearing witness to what happened to Job. It was happening to me. My spirit said, "Have you seen my servant, Brother Vernon?"

I knew it was going to take all that God had put in me to overcome this challenge. The different medications to slow my heart rate were taking a toll on me.

On February 23, 2018, we learned my wife's nephew wasn't taking his medication, and he had disappeared on the streets of Petersburg, Virginia, was homeless, and had other challenging issues.

During this time, my wife spent time in the emergency room due to everything that was going on. My wife and I were saying, "Lord, you must be getting ready to bless us abundantly." The tremendous pressure of the spiritual battle taking place was centered on making us disrespect God by not following what his word says to do. But I remembered the words the Lord had spoken to me, "It's already done."

We had to continue to pray, praise God, worship God and be led by the Holy Spirit. We knew the car accident, my heart procedure, and my wife's nephew's situations were just the start of the process. We still had bills, I was out of work, and my leave time was running out.

But God said it was "already done." My wife and I recited Mathew 28:20: (KJV) "Teaching them to observe all things whatsoever I have commanded you: and, lo, I am with you always, even unto the end of the world. Amen."

Jesus will be with us until the end of the world. Matthew 19:26 (KJV) says, "But Jesus beheld them, and said unto them, With men this is impossible; but with God all things are possible."

Our faith rests in God. We are assured and confident in John 14:21. (MSG) "The person who knows my commandments and keeps them, that's who loves me. And the person who loves me will be loved by my Father, and I will love him and make myself plain to him."

It was plain to my wife and I that the greater the challenge, the greater the victory. Death could not touch me because of my relationship with God my Father and the personal dreams he had shown me.

In visions and dreams, he showed me the Lord's coming not once but three times, and I was part of each one. In one dream I was watching the church being caught up in the air: there was a presence beside me showing me myself in the mist with others being caught up with Jesus. But deep inside I knew there was more to come. I had to pick up my bed and walk, enduring and following through on what was said and shown to me.

My Father God is greater than any situation. On March 12, 2018, I was scheduled for my 1st heart procedure that would slow down my heart rhythm.

My wife and I had already prayed, and Brother Norton and his wife, Elder Lynch, and church members at Mt. Gilead prayed too.

But my wife and I were flowing with the message that we had received from the Lord: "It's already done." Praise God! I had the procedure done, and afterward, the nurse asked me if I needed morphine for pain. I told her I wasn't in any pain. Hallelujah!

I was well on my way to recovery when, on March 19, 2018, a lady ran into the back of our car and injured my wife. I remembered the Lord's message to me, but now I heard another message: "For we wrestle not against flesh and blood, but principalities, against powers, against the rulers of darkness of this world, against spiritual wickedness in high places" (Ephesians 6:12 KJV).

The devil was defeated, and death has lost its sting. We will live forever with Christ Jesus.

On March 22, 2018, my wife's job would not allow

her to leave to see the doctor. On April 8, after leaving the morning church service, my wife missed another accident when a tractor trailer went over the overpass on 288 and crashed on Route 10. My Father God himself is covering us.

On April 10, 2018, my credit card was fraudulently charged. I was awakened by a chime to check my cell phone and saw the email from the bank. Now, from December 30, 2017, until April 10, 2018, the Lord said there was a flow with him. The way we serve him in our lives every day, but while we do that there is an enter listening to hearing his voice.

Exodus 4:21 (KJV) says, "And the Lord said unto Moses, When thou goest to return into Egypt, see that thou do all those wonders before Pharaoh, which I have put in thine hand: but I will harden his heart, that he shall not let the people go."

Exodus 7:3 (KJV): "And I will harden Pharaoh's heart, and multiply my signs and my wonders in the land of Egypt."

Exodus 14:4 (KJV): "And I will harden Pharaoh's heart that he shall follow after them; and I will be honored upon Pharaoh, and upon all his host; that the Egyptians may know that I *am* the Lord. And they did so."

These are for his glory. But we must be "wise as serpents, and harmless as doves" (Matthew 10:16 KJV). The spirit of discernment is key with the leading of the spirit of truth. We miss the spirit of truth when we do not discern properly.

As it says in 1 Peter 1:21 (KJV), "For the prophecy came not in old time by the will of man: but holy men of God spake *as they were* moved by the Holy Ghost."

The key is holy men of God, men who were inspired by God himself. Discerning the truth of end time pastors, teachers and preachers. We must flow and walk in the flow with God, which leads to an inner flow when the waters are troubled, you can step in and receive everything you need.

Over the next seven months I was still being challenged physically and financially.

In October 22, 2018, I had to have a 2nd heart procedure called cardioversion, which was more extensive then the first procedure, and I was under anesthesia for four or five hours.

I still believed what the Lord had told me: "It's already done." But going through the procedure wasn't easy. I had some complications with bleeding and chest pain. They went through both my legs to my heart.

The Lord is still good—I give the devil no place here—Jesus is the healer! Amen. Now, right now, I am going all in for Jesus.

Mark 9:23 (KJV) says, "Jesus said unto him, If thou canst believe, all things are possible to him that believeth." Did you hear what Jesus just said? If you can believe, then all things are possible.

The question to ask is, believe what? If you can believe that Christ is the Son of God and that God sent his son to die for us, then all things are possible (John 3:16). If you can believe that there is no other name under heaven by which men can be saved (Acts 4:12), then all things are possible. If you can believe the word God spoke to you and you only. The key is what has God spoken to you lately.

We must always remember everything centers on what Christ has already done for us. The price has already been paid in full. The journey must still continue because it is already done. Hallelujah! The 3rd heart procedure was done through my wrist to the lower part of my heart. God has strengthen me through my experience with him during the time of the accident. This is my joy, relationship with the Father.

On November 9, 2018, my wife was involved in another accident. The car was total and she had to have surgery on her back March 28, 2019. Now, she was out of work and dealing with not being able to walk. This will pass too. I will not give-up, I will not bow-down, Christ is true and forever. Come hell, high water, low water and no water; I will only submit to the living word of God.

Chapter Three

We Wrestle Not against Flesh and Blood

Ephesians 6:12 (KJV) says, "For we wrestle not against flesh and blood, but against principalities, against powers, against the rulers of the darkness of this world, against spiritual wickedness in high places."

In Greek, "principalities" means ruler or chief. These principalities are ruling demonic spirits possessing authority over different governments in the world. These powers usually involve nations, people, and different races.

I believe one of the highest principalities is death. There are many unseen dark forces against Christians in the world, but God ordered his angels to protect us.

On December 30, 2017, I had an encounter with death. I now believe that if my life had been filled with anything other than God, I would not be here today. These demonic forces are here to stop Christians from fulfilling what God has promised us.

When God showed me the Lord's coming in visions and dreams three times, he spoke to me and said it was more than a dream. He said it was a promise. Praise God!

Matthew 8:5-10 (KJV) says:

> And when Jesus was entered into Capernaum, there came unto him a centurion, beseeching him, And saying, Lord, my servant lieth at

> home sick of the palsy, grievously tormented. And Jesus saith unto him, I will come and heal him. The centurion answered and said, Lord, I am not worthy that thou shouldest come under my roof: but speak the word only, and my servant shall be healed.
>
> For I am a man under authority, having soldiers under me: and I say to this man, Go, and he goeth; and to another, Come, and he cometh; and to my servant, Do this, and he doeth it. When Jesus heard it, he marveled, and said to them that followed, Verily I say unto you, I have not found so great faith, no, not in Israel.

Praise God!

The centurion told Jesus if he spoke the word, only he knew his servant would be healed. I believe when times are challenging us, we must have a word of God in us to draw on at that time. We as Christians must only speak God's word. The word can be from the Bible, or from God, if he has spoken to you, as he did to me.

In the accident, God spoke to me and said, "It's already done. Pick up your bed and walk."

I knew in my spirit it was a process I had to go through, and God was on my side. When God spoke it, the victory was already completed. God knows the end from the beginning, and nothing is hidden from him. When God speaks, powerful words come fourth.

When God speaks, we must obey. The spirit of truth is getting us ready for end-time discernment.

John 6:63 (KJV) says, "It is the spirit that quickeneth; the flesh profiteth nothing: the words that I speak unto you, they are spirit, and they are life."

Jesus said the words he speaks to you. These words are life and spirit. Stay focused on your course, and let the Holy Spirit direct your path.

Chapter Four

Basic Ingredients

I'd like to share some basic ingredients from my first book. First, prayer and fasting bring a Christian to the point of total submission to God and to His presence. It enables Christians to be more sensitive and hear what the Holy Spirit is saying to them.

Direction is given in the first step, which, if not done, causes everything else to be placed on hold. God has an action plan, which involves Christians acting in faith on what God shows or speaks to them.

David fasted, and in Isaiah 58:6 (KJV), it says, "Is not this the fast that I have chosen? to loose the bands of wickedness, to undo the heavy burdens, and to let the oppressed go free, and that ye break every yoke?"

God tells Christians what type of fast He wants. Luke 18:1 (KJV) says, "And he spake a parable unto them to this end, that men ought always to pray, and not to faint."

Jesus tells Christians to pray always. It makes Christians more sensitive to God and the teachings of the Holy Spirit. We must have a listening ear to hear from God. Second Timothy 2:15 says, "Study to shew thyself approved unto God, a workman that needeth not to be ashamed, rightly dividing the word of truth" (KJV).

Our study habits and how we learn prove our faithfulness to God. The process of learning never ends, and the God in us always increases. Christians must be taught and their minds renewed with the word of God, according to Romans 12:2 (KJV): "And be not conformed to this world: but be ye transformed by the renewing of your mind, that ye may prove what is that good, and acceptable, and perfect, will of God." Praise God!

Serving God is a continuous act. The way you believe in God has a lot to do with what you receive from him. Also, the learning and maturing processes begin with a good church home, which is grounded in the local church taught by anointed ministers.

Finding a good church home means visiting different churches, but your spirit will bear witness with one.

I believe the most important aspect of your faith is applying God's word in your life. When Christians actually apply the word, it becomes more effective. James 1:22 (KJV) says, "But be ye doers of the word, and not hearers only, deceiving your own selves."

Christians cannot merely listen to what is being preached but must actively apply the word. Many Christians listen yet do nothing. A church might hold ten thousand members, but you may only find two thousand doing the work. God doesn't only work in the church but outside as well.

Relationships are give and take, which requires responsibilities of both parties. There are some things that God will do because he loves us. However, there many blessings God has already bestowed, beginning with Christ dying on the cross for us. God loved us before we loved him.

God's love is great. Malachi 3:8 (KJV) says, "Will a man rob God? Yet ye have robbed me. But ye say, Wherein have we robbed thee? In tithes and offerings." This tells Christians to bring tithes to the church so God will bless you. Relationship is the key in which God matures and guides us. God is the tithe.

Tithing is a process that never stops. God increases us, and we increase our tithes. The question is, does God need our money? No!

Deuteronomy 10:9 says, (KJV) "Wherefore Levi hath no part nor inheritance with his brethren; the Lord is his inheritance, according as the Lord thy God promised him."

Did you hear what the Lord said? He will be their

inheritance. Glory to God! Our Father is everything you will ever need. God is healing, deliverance, love, compassion, prosperity, patience, goodness, kindness, and whatever else you can think of. That's him. Praise God!

Chapter Five

God's Way

Psalm 103:7 (KJV) says, "He made known his ways unto Moses, his acts unto the children of Israel."

Just like in a marriage: as time goes on, you begin to know your spouse's ways of doing things. Amen!

The marriage grows and becomes a unity of oneness. The question is, do you know God's ways, or do you just know his acts or deeds?

I remember the first years of our marriage, when I was meditating on his word. I asked God about divorce and what was considered a divorce. I had a list, asking what if she did this? and what if this happens? The more questions I asked, the more God showed me myself. He showed every hole I was in and how I had gotten out. I had to look at myself and forgive, as he forgave me. My questions stopped because I realized God is the greatest forgiver, and I must follow his example.

First Corinthians 13:5 (AMP) says, "It is not conceited (arrogant and inflated with pride); it is not rude (unmannerly) *and* does not act unbecomingly. Love (God's love in us) does not insist on its own rights *or* its own way, *for* it is not self-seeking; it is not touchy *or* fretful *or* resentful; it takes no account of the evil done to it [it pays no attention to a suffered wrong]."

Walking in agape love—the love of God. When

something is done wrong to you and you take no account of it, that's agape love. Praise God! It's God's way of doing things. The manner and type of love God has shown on us. God gave his only son for us.

Our relationship with him brings us to this kind of love. In these end times, we must be fully in operation with God. We must get back to our first love. Remember when you first came to him? Remember the freshness, and the going all out when doing everything for him? The newness was like buying a new car and trying out all the gadgets. This must happen again.

Jesus didn't say this was how you'll know these are my disciples; instead, you'll learn by great preaching and teaching, great miracles and wonders, and great healings and manifestations; by speaking in tongues or not speaking in tongues, or by casting out devils and receiving a gift.

But John 13:34–35 (KJV) says, "A new commandment I give unto you, That ye love one another; as I have loved you, that ye also love one another. By this shall all men know that ye are my disciples, if ye have love one to another." It's the love that we have for one another, which makes the difference.

Jesus says this is how you'll know they're his disciples.

Glory to God! End times produce a generation that is not self-centered. A time is already here now that we Christians must reveal our true nature. We belong to God no matter what happens.

The battle is spiritual and not natural, so use everything God has blessed you with—all your gifts and talents for his kingdom. God is our inheritance and everything we will ever need. Speaking the word through our mouth is also key.

In August 2018, my wife, Gerri, was out shopping. She was driving to a store when her back began to hurt. She started to scratch her back with her nails and encountered a bump. She scratched it and thought no more about it.

Upon entering the store, an employee noticed that the back of her blouse was soaked in blood. The employee took her to the back and use the first aid kit. It didn't stop the bleeding. My wife drove to the emergency room. While on the way, she called me at work. I immediately spoke to that bleeding and commanded it to stop in Jesus's name. We took authority over this situation.

She arrived at the ER, and the first thing the nurse said was that the bleeding had stopped. Praise God!

They put a bandage on the spot and released her. How good is God? He is present with us, even when it feels like he is miles away. God's ways of doing things.

Chapter Six

The Comeback: Devil, You Are a Liar

In any sports comeback, it takes an internal force to come back and win. In my college football days, we played Hampton University for their homecoming in Hampton, Virginia. Here we are, Bowie State University, down twenty-one to zero at halftime. All kinds of thoughts went through our minds, but our will, determination, and what we believe determined the outcome. We came back to beat Hampton University twenty-eight to twenty-one on their home field.

The head coach gave the team a speech at halftime, which was quite simple yet challenged the team. He said, "What did you come down here to do?"

As I remember my car accident from December 30, 2017, my three heart procedures, my wife's nephew's situation, a second accident involving my wife and I, and then a third accident where my wife was hit from behind (in which the car was totaled), I realized God has stacked the deck against the enemy.

The words spoken to me from the beginning—"It's already done; pick up your bed and walk"—have made me realize no matter what you're going through, it's what the scripture says and what is revealed by the Holy Spirit that counts.

Matthew 1:23 (KJV) says, "Behold, a virgin shall be

with child, and shall bring forth a son, and they shall call his name Emmanuel, which being interpreted is, God with us."

No matter what force might be against you, God is with us. Emmanuel is the word. Our determination, faith, and obedience to the Lord will always bring me through any situation. Three heart procedures, three accidents and numerous challenges can never defeat us. God has already spoken the words to us. Just stay tuned for The "Comeback, God Is Not Finished With You Yet."

The Salvation Prayer

This is perhaps the most important part of the book. If you have not received Jesus Christ as your Lord and Savior, you can do so right now. It is the beginning of the relationship, which puts you in position to receive from God.

Together we pray: Lord Jesus, you are the Christ and the Son of the living God. I believe with all my heart that God raised you from the dead. I call on your name right now, Lord Jesus. Come into my heart. I receive you now and make you Lord and Savior of my life. I thank you, heavenly Father, for giving me the Son. In Jesus's name, I pray. Amen.

Welcome to the body of Christ!

Start your daily commitment to Christ. It's a relationship that requires you to listen to the voice of God. It's a two-way relationship. We talk to him and he talks to us. Glory to God! You are now a new creature in Christ Jesus, according to the scripture (2 Corinthians 5:17).

Be blessed.

About the Author

Vernon M. Henderson is the founder of the Jericho Leadership Institute and a member of Mt. Gilead Full Gospel International Ministries in Richmond, Virginia. In October 1989, Brother Henderson rededicated his life to Christ and started his journey with the Lord. He and Geraldine fellowshipped for two years before they got married in January 1998. They've had a blessed twenty-three years together and look forward to growing young in the Lord.

Brother Henderson works for Chesterfield Juvenile Detention Home as a shift coordinator. While working night shifts, his dedication and determination to serve the Lord became fruitful.

He attended the Richmond Christian Center Bible Institute and School of Ministry in Richmond, Virginia, where he majored in Christian counseling; he attended

Bowie State University and in 2006 finished his Bachelor of Science degree in Criminal Justice from Bluefield College. He earned his Master of Arts degree in Christian Leadership Studies from Liberty Baptist Theological Seminary in 2010.

He has served in prison ministry since 1994, helping restore incarcerated offenders back to their communities. In 2015 he received word from the Lord to take a position at Prince William County Juvenile Detention Center.

Mr. Henderson started working midnights as a team leader but eventually move to a day shift. God blessed him with being promoted to shift supervisor on that team. At that time he was involved in the accident that forever changed his life and mind-set about God.